CHRIS SPROUSE

TOM STRONG
COLLECTED EDITION
BOOK 4

ALAN MOORE
writer

PETER HOGAN
writer

GEOFF JOHNS
writer

JERRY ORDWAY
penciller

CHRIS SPROUSE
penciller

KARL STORY
inker

JOHN PAUL LEON
artist

AMERICA'S
BEST COMICS

**TREVOR SCOTT
RICHARD FRIEND
SANDRA HOPE
JOHN DELL
JERRY ORDWAY**
additional inks

TODD KLEIN
lettering, logos
& design

**DAVE STEWART
WILDSTORM FX**
coloring

TOM STRONG
created by Alan Moore
& Chris Sprouse

JIM LEE
Editorial Director

JOHN NEE
VP —Business Development

SCOTT DUNBIER
Executive Editor

KRISTY QUINN
Assistant Editor

WRITER **JASON AARON**

ARTIST **R.M. GUÉRA**

COLORIST **GIULIA BRUSCO**   LETTERERS **PHIL BALSMAN** AND **STEVE WANDS**

SCALPED

CASINO BOOGIE

PRAIRIE ROSE

INDIAN RESERVATION

19 miles

Original series covers by
JOCK

Introduction by
GARTH ENNIS

SCALPED created by
JASON AARON and R.M. GUÉRA

KAREN BERGER
Senior VP-Executive Editor

WILL DENNIS
Editor-original series

CASEY SEIJAS
Assistant Editor-original series

BOB HARRAS
Editor-collected edition

ROBBIN BROSTERMAN
Senior Art Director

PAUL LEVITZ
President & Publisher

GEORG BREWER
VP-Design & DC Direct Creative

RICHARD BRUNING
Senior VP-Creative Director

PATRICK CALDON
Executive VP-Finance &
Operations

CHRIS CARAMALIS
VP-Finance

JOHN CUNNINGHAM
VP-Marketing

TERRI CUNNINGHAM
VP-Managing Editor

ALISON GILL
VP-Manufacturing

DAVID HYDE
VP-Publicity

HANK KANALZ
VP-General Manager, WildStorm

JIM LEE
Editorial Director-WildStorm

PAULA LOWITT
Senior VP-Business & Legal Affairs

MARYELLEN MCLAUGHLIN
VP-Advertising &
Custom Publishing

JOHN NEE
Senior VP-Business Development

GREGORY NOVECK
Senior VP-Creative Affairs

SUE POHJA
VP-Book Trade Sales

STEVE ROTTERDAM
Senior VP-Sales & Marketing

CHERYL RUBIN
Senior VP-Brand Management

JEFF TROJAN
VP-Business Development,
DC Direct

BOB WAYNE
VP-Sales

SCALPED-CASINO BOOGIE

Logo design and cover illustration by JOCK
Publication design by BRAINCHILD STUDIOS/NYC
Published by DC Comics. Cover, introduction and compilation
Copyright © 2008 DC Comics. All Rights Reserved.

DC Comics, 1700 Broadway, New York, NY 10019
A Warner Bros. Entertainment Company.
Printed in Canada. Second Printing.
ISBN: 978-1-4012-1654-2

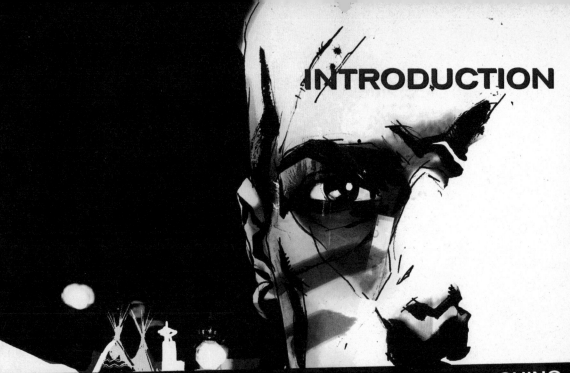

INTRODUCTION

They're pretty few and far between in comic books, mind you. Oh, don't get me wrong, plenty of capable new writers appear every year, but most of them are happy knocking out superhero stories. Those are the industry's bread and butter, and some good work's been done on them over the years. But ultimately it comes down to playing with toys: the characters that you read as a kid (or some variation thereon), that you finally have a chance to write yourself. Nice, warm, glowing dollop of nostalgia.

What's a little harder is coming up with toys of your own. Making them stick. And making them sing, come to that, because the superhero genre holds no monopoly on self-repetition. So when somebody pops up and manages all those tricks with some style, those of us who care about such things tend to take notice.

A while ago there was Brian Azzarello, who arrived with the crime book to end them all, 100 BULLETS. Then came Brian Vaughan with EX and Y, and all of a sudden I was reading monthly comics again, not just collections and miniseries. And now there's Jason Aaron, following his excellent debut THE OTHER SIDE with the object of this particular exercise: SCALPED. Hmmm...notice how they're all Yanks? I remember a time when—oh, never mind. Forget it.

Two things slowly occurred to me as I was reading SCALPED – slowly, because I was so engrossed that it took some effort to pause long enough for analytical thought. First off, the sheer confidence that comes across in the storytelling – both in Jason's writing and R.M. Guéra's dry-as-dust artwork – is actually quite staggering. Just a few episodes in, and these guys have their game locked down in a way that most writers and artists take years to achieve. Second, this is a crime story, all right (a neo-western/political/historical/Native/ultra-violent/black comedy crime story, to be precise), but it's not relying on any of the usual props from other genres for its survival. None of the aforementioned super-types, no horror, no fantasy or sci-fi, nothing. Not an elf or an angel in sight. And for an adult-imprint monthly in the current sales climate, that's both refreshing and pretty bloody brave.

How Jason can hit the ground running like this is beyond me. It could be in the genes, I suppose, given that his cousin was Gustav Hasford—writer of *The Short Timers*, which you may know of as *Full Metal Jacket*, and the even better *The Phantom Blooper* (mind you, my great-grandfather ran the local temperance society, so I've always been a bit doubtful about the genetic argument). However he's done it, SCALPED is nothing short of a triumph, a little gem of a book that I hope goes from strength to strength.

So if you enjoy this second collection of the best new series in years, by all means spread the word. Tell your friends, your family, the people you owe money to. Talk about it. Blog about it. Do whatever you can to help this book survive until its natural conclusion, so that we can all of us watch the fun, every step of the way.

Because Jason Aaron is a writer worth watching. And SCALPED is a book worth fighting for.

GARTH ENNIS
October 2007

GARTH ENNIS is the co-creator of PREACHER, HITMAN, *Wormwood*, WAR STORY and *303*, and the current writer of *The Punisher* for Marvel Comics. He is also writing *The Boys, Dan Dare, Streets of Glory* and a new horror book, *Crossed*. He lives in New York City with his wife, Ruth.

HANDED 'EM OFF TO RED CROW'S BOYS. FIGURED THAT WAS THE LAST I'D EVER SEE OF *HIS* ASS...

...BUT WOULD YA BELIEVE THE SLIPPERY BASTARD UP AND GOT AWAY AGAIN?

I'M GONNA NEED YOU TO GO *BACK* TO YOUR FRIENDS, MACK, WAIT AND SEE IF HE CONTACTS ANY--

WAIT! WHAT THE FUCK DO YOU MEAN, HE GOT AWAY?

I MEAN SOMETHING HAPPENED AND HE GOT AWAY.

DON'T ASK ME, I WAS IN THE SHITTER.

OH CHRIST, I'M *DEAD.* HE'S GONNA KNOW IT WAS ME.

LOOK, *CALM DOWN.* YOU GOT ARRESTED WITH EVERYONE ELSE, RIGHT? HOW THEY GONNA KNOW IT WAS YOU WHO RATTED THEM OUT?

AND WHAT'S THE BIG DEAL ANYWAY? IT'S NOT LIKE YOU GUYS WERE PLANNIN' THE LINDBERGH KIDNAPPING OR NOTHIN', RIGHT?

THE *WHAT?*

NEVER MIND.

NONE OF US HAD A CLUE WHAT THE PLAN WAS SUPPOSED TO BE, JUST THAT WE WAS HITTIN' THE CASINO TONIGHT.

THAT WHITEBOY HAD US ALL SO SCARED, WE'D DO ANYTHING HE SAID. HE'S FUCKIN' *PSYCHO.*

CHAPTER TWO

DOWN ON THE KILLIN' FLOOR

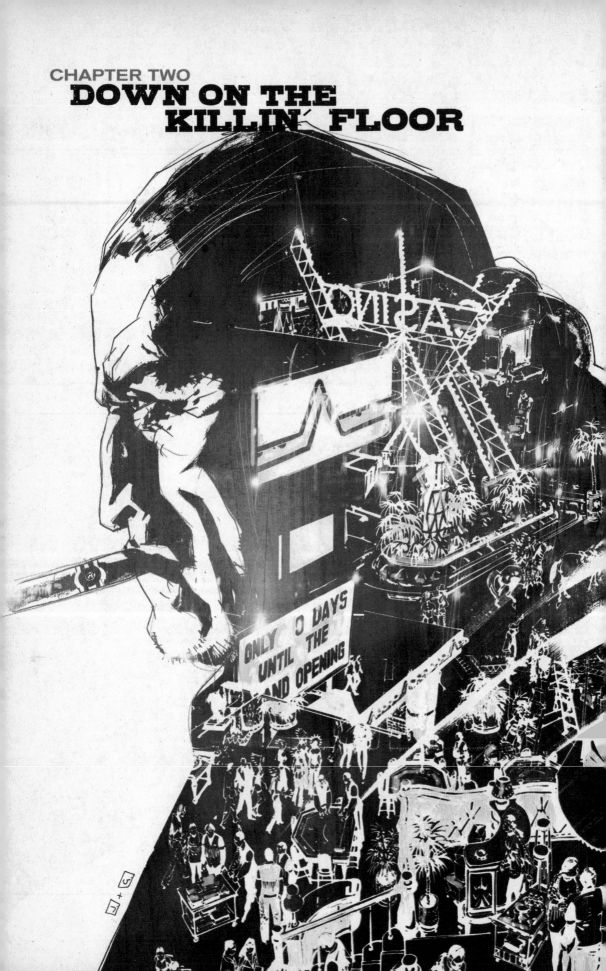

THIRTEEN MINUTES LATER...

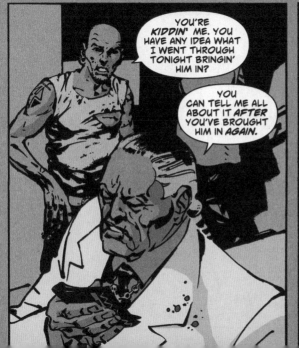

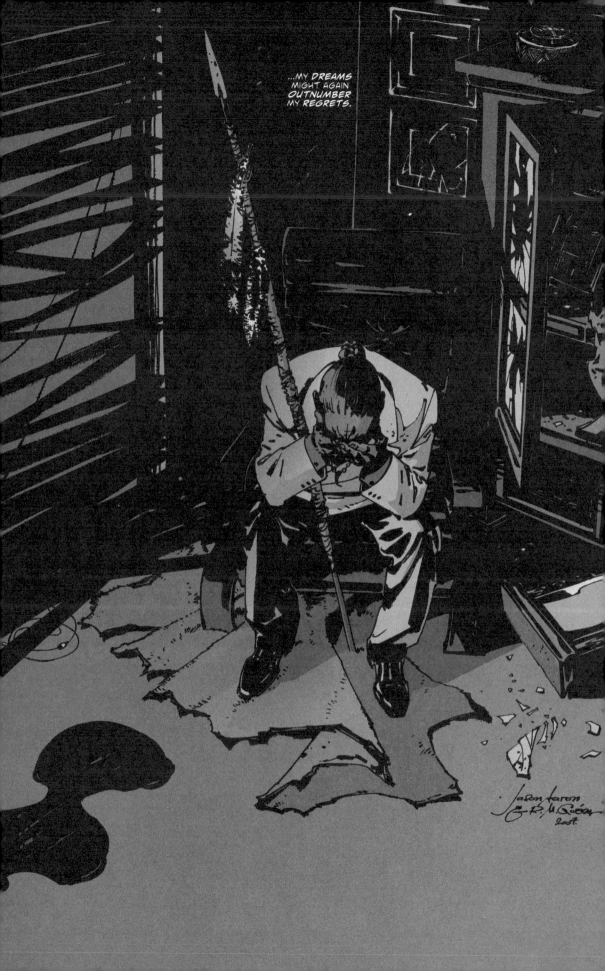

...MY DREAMS MIGHT AGAIN OUTNUMBER MY REGRETS.

SO... ANYBODY KNOW WHAT THE HELL WE'RE DOIN' HERE?

I JUST GOT A MESSAGE TO MEET UP. SOMETHIN' TO DO WITH THE CASINO'S GRAND OPENING.

WHERE'S GINA BAD HORSE?

SKREECH

GINA LEFT TOWN YESTERDAY. SAID SHE WOULDN'T BE BACK FOR A COUPLA WEEKS.

There Are Two Kinds Of Pedestrians QUICK & DEAD MY HEROES HAVE ALWAYS KILLED COWBOYS DIESEL

WELL, THEN WHO THE HELL CALLED THIS MEETING?

OOOF!

YOU'RE FOOLIN' YOURSELF IF YA THINK YA CAN *BEAT* ME, BAD HORSE.

YOU'RE *RIGHT*, DIESEL. YOU'RE THE REAL FUCKIN' DEAL.

YOU'RE BETTER'N ME AT *KUNG FU* AND *KNIFE FIGHTIN'* AND *ALL A'* THAT SHIT.

PROBLY GOT A BIGGER *COCK* TOO.

BUT YA KNOW, THERE IS STILL JUST THAT ONE TEENSY LITTLE THING WHERE I *KNOW* I GOT A LEG UP ON YA...

...AND THERE AIN'T *NOTHIN'* YA CAN *EVER* FUCKIN' DO ABOUT IT.

YA SEE, ME?...

I'M *A REAL* INDIAN.

YOU'VE BLOWN OUT
YOUR *KNEE* BEFORE,
HAVEN'T YOU?

YEARS AGO.
FOOTBALL, I'D
GUESS.

WHERE'D YOU
LEARN *KARATE?* A
CORRESPONDENCE
COURSE?

CHAPTER FOUR
A THUNDER BEING
NATION I AM

IF ANYTHING HAPPENS TO HER, LINCOLN, I PROMISE YOU...I'LL COME BACK HERE...

AND YOU AND ME, WE'LL BE GOIN' UP TOGETHER TO MEET THE GREAT MYSTERY.

DON'T COME BACK HERE, CATCHER.

EVER.

WHAT?

WHAT THE HELL'RE YOU STARING AT?

I'M STARIN' AT YOU, LINCOLN RED CROW...

IT'S JUS' SO GODDAMN GOOD TO SEE YA AGAIN.

AFTER ALL THIS TIME, WHY YOU WANNA GO CHASIN' AFTER *GINA BAD HORSE* AGAIN?

YOU *DO* REMEMBER WHAT HAPPENED THE LAST TIME YOU TWO SPOKE, DON'T YA?

I'M HAVIN' *VISIONS* AGAIN, GRANNY. MESSAGES FROM THE *THUNDER BEINGS* OF THE WEST.

WAKINYAN TOLD ME GINA'S GONNA *DIE*, UNLESS I DO SOMETHIN' TO STOP IT.

I TOLD YA BEFORE, CATCHER, JUST 'CAUSE YOU GOT DRUNK AND STARTED SEEIN' THINGS, THAT *DON'T* MEAN YOU HAD NO VISION.

YOU SHOULDN'T OUGHTTA BANDY ABOUT TALK OF *WAKINYAN* AND *HEYOKAS* LIKE YOU DO.

YOU STILL BELIEVE YOU CAN SEE PEOPLE'S *ANIMAL TOTEMS*?

COME SEE ME AGAIN WHEN YOU'RE *ON THE WAGON*, AND THEN WE'LL TALK.

I'M JUST TRYING TO HELP AN OLD FRIEND, GRANNY.

YOU EVER THINK MAYBE GINA DON'T NEED YOUR HELP? YOU KNOW HER *SON'S* BACK ON THE REZ NOW, RIGHT?

YEAH, I THINK I HEARD THAT. MAYBE I'LL GET A CHANCE TO CHAT WITH HIM, TOO.

"BUT I RECKON IT'LL COME TO ME."

12:32 AM.

ONE OF THE MOST IMPORTANT ROLES IN LAKOTA SOCIETY IS THAT OF *HEYOKA*, THE SACRED CLOWN OR THUNDER DREAMER.

HEYOKA IS A LAKOTA WAY OF BEING, A *MEDICINE WAY*.

A PERSON IS CALLED TO BE HEYOKA BY WAKINYAN, THE THUNDER BEING, THE ONE WHO IS MANY.

≷BRRRIIING≷

AND WHEN A *VISION* COMES FROM WAKINYAN...

HELLO?

BRRRIIIING⋇

WAKINYAN LIVES IN A LODGE AT THE EDGE OF THE WORLD WHERE THE SUN GOES DOWN. HIS VOICE IS THE THUNDERCLAP. THE GLANCE OF HIS EYE IS LIGHTNING.

LOOK HERE, CATCHER. WHY DON'T YOU JUST *FORGET* THIS FOOL NOTION A' GOING TO THE CASINO.

COME INSIDE, HAVE A BISCUIT AND SOME SORGHUM. TELL ME ABOUT THIS VISION OF YOURS AND MAYBE WE CAN WORK IT OUT TOGETHER.

AFRAID I CAN'T DO THAT, GRANNY.

I ALWAYS THOUGHT YOU WERE *THE ONE*, YA KNOW.

GINA, BLESS HER SOUL, COULD NEVER KEEP HER OWN FAMILY TOGETHER, LET ALONE A WHOLE MOVEMENT.

AND RED CROW YOU COULD TELL WAS ALWAYS LOOKIN' FOR SLAVES MORE THAN FOLLOWERS.

BUT *YOU*... YOU COULDA BEEN THE *LEADER* WE ALL NEEDED.

YOU COULDA DONE SOME *GOOD*.

I WAS *THERE*, WASN'T I? I DID MY PART! I TOOK A DAMN BULLET!

THAT WAS *THIRTY YEARS AGO!* WHERE YOU BEEN SINCE THEN?!

LIVING IN THAT TRAILER IN THE MIDDLE OF NOWHERE, DRUNK OUTTA YER GOURD, TALKING TO THAT GODDAMN HORSE...!

1:15 AM.

"MY TASK IS DONE, MY SONG HATH CEASED, MY THEME HAS DIED INTO AN ECHO."

THIS IS THE STORY OF A MAN THE WORLD CALLS *CATCHER*.

"IT IS FIT THE SPELL SHOULD BREAK OFF THIS PROTRACTED DREAM. THE TORCH SHALL BE EXTINGUISH'D WHICH HATH LIT MY MIDNIGHT LAMP--AND WHAT IS WRIT, IS WRIT."

BORN 1952 IN WEST CHESTER, PENNSYLVANIA.

Wheat Beer

OXFORD GRADUATE. RHODES SCHOLAR.

CAPTAIN OF THE EQUESTRIAN TEAM.

"WOULD IT WERE WORTHIER! BUT I AM NOT NOW THAT WHICH I HAVE BEEN, AND MY VISIONS FLIT LESS PALPABLY BEFORE ME..."

LOVER OF WORDSWORTH, BYRON AND THE BRITISH ROMANTICS..

ACQUITTED MURDERER.

"AND THE GLOW WHICH IN MY SPIRIT DWELT IS FLUTTERING, FAINT, AND... LOW."

CHAPTER SIX

REQUIEM FOR A DOG SOLDIER

FBI

SPECIAL AGENT

jock—07

RENO, NEVADA.

Pink Flamingo MOTOR LODGE

VACANCY

VACANCY

42

DO NOT DISTURB

...TUNING IN TO CHANNEL 12 ACTION NEWS. COMING UP LATER, PEG JANSEN TELLS US ABOUT A LOCAL COOKING SCHOOL THAT'S CREATING QUITE A STIR.

TO DATE ONLY ONE SUSPECT HAS BEEN APPREHENDED: JOHN RAYFIELD BUSTILL, ALSO KNOWN AS LINCOLN RED CROW, WHO WAS CAPTURED TWO WEEKS AGO WHILE TRYING TO CROSS THE BORDER INTO CANADA.

MR. BUSTILL WAS ARRAIGNED TODAY ON DOUBLE MURDER CHARGES AND AWAITS TRIAL IN RAPID CITY.

SOURCES WITHIN THE FBI REPORT THAT AGENTS MAY BE CLOSE TO TRACKING DOWN AT LEAST ONE OF THE REMAINING SUSPECTS, BUT NO WORD YET ON...

BUT FIRST, THE NATIONWIDE MANHUNT CONTINUES FOR MEMBERS OF THE RADICAL AMERICAN INDIAN GROUP SUSPECTED OF SHOOTING AND KILLING TWO FEDERAL AGENTS A YEAR AGO ON THE PRAIRIE ROSE RESERVATION IN SOUTH DAKOTA.

YOU WEREN'T THERE, LORA. IT WAS A *WAR ZONE* ON THAT REZ BACK THEN. FOR THREE YEARS, WE HAD THE HIGHEST MURDER RATE PER CAPITA IN THE UNITED STATES.

WHY? SIMPLY BECAUSE THOSE OF US IN THE DOG SOLDIER SOCIETY DARED TO STAND UP FOR OUR OWN CULTURE AND RIGHTS.

WE DARED TO OPPOSE THE CORPORATE BANKS AND THE URANIUM MINERS AND THE CHRISTIAN CHURCHES. AND FOR THAT, THE FEDS AND SOME IN OUR OWN TRIBAL GOVERNMENT WANTED TO SEE EVERY SINGLE ONE OF US EITHER DEAD OR IN JAIL.

ALL WE HAD WAS EACH OTHER. IT WAS A *SACRED* BOND, AND NOTHING CAN EVER--

OH *SPARE* ME! I'VE HEARD THIS SAME BULLSHIT A THOUSAND TIMES, FROM YOU AND LAWRENCE BOTH. I DON'T GIVE A DAMN ABOUT YOUR LITTLE CLUB AND ITS SECRET HANDSHAKES...

I JUST DON'T WANNA SEE MY BROTHER *DIE* IN A GODDAMN JAIL CELL!

NEITHER DO *I*, DAMNIT!

SURE. SURE YOU DON'T...

BUT BETTER HIM THAN *YOU*, RIGHT?

DON'T EVER COME HERE AGAIN, GINA.

TWO DAYS AGO.

"OH GOD, I DON'T WANNA DIE... NOT LIKE THIS... PLEASE..."

IF YOU DON'T WANNA DIE, THEN STOP YOUR DAMN *WHINING* AND TELL ME WHAT THE *HELL* YOU'RE DOING PROWLIN' AROUND OUT HERE!

GINA...

GINA, ARE YOU *CRAZY?* THESE GUYS ARE THE *FBI.*

SHUT UP, LAWRENCE! I KNOW WHAT I'M DOING.

YOU DON'T KNOW *SHIT,* YOU STUPID *BITCH...*

TONIGHT.

HELLO?

LAWRENCE, I JUST WANTED YOU TO KNOW, I'M TAKING CARE OF EVERYTHING. I KNOW EXACTLY WHAT HAS TO BE DONE.

WHAT ARE YOU TALKING ABOUT, GINA?

I'M GOING TO SEE HIM.

HIM WHO?

THE ONLY MAN ALIVE WHO CAN GET YOU OUT OF THERE.

GINA...

THERE'S NO OTHER WAY, LAWRENCE. I HAVE TO DO THIS.

NO, YOU DON'T.

WHERE ARE YOU? ARE YOU STILL IN TOWN?

NO, I LEFT YESTERDAY. I HAD THIS DREAM... AND IT... IT'S ALL CLEAR TO ME NOW, LAWRENCE. THERE'S ONLY ONE WAY TO SAVE YOU.